Not in Otter's Pocket

Written by Suzanne Senior
Illustrated by Angelika Scudamore

Collins

Sea Otter had a smooth rock. He twirled it. He played with it.

He kept it in his armpit pocket.

"It's the best rock I have ever seen!" he said.

One day, Otter went swimming.

He jumped in and swam.

Then he peeped in his pocket.

“My rock is not here!” he cried. “I must have lost it”.

Otter looked all across the beach.

The rock was not there.

He scooped up a pink rock.
It looked about right.

Dear me!

It was not a rock. It was a crab!

“Ouch!” yelled Otter. “This is sharp.”

Otter looked stern.

"I do not like sharp things in my pocket," he said.

Otter pushed around in some seaweed.

He spotted a bright blue rock.

Dear me!

It was not a rock. It was an urchin!

Otter squeaked, "This is sharp, too!"

He frowned and put it down.

"I do not like sharp things in my pocket," he complained.

Next, Otter peeped into a pool.

He found a little, brown rock.

Dear me!

It was not a rock. It was a sea snail!

Otter yelped, “This has lots of gloop!”

He set the snail free.

“I do not like gloop in my pocket,”
he groaned.

Otter dried his tears.

Then, he spotted a rock ...

"My best rock!" Otter shouted.

He started twirling it.
He started playing with it.

He tucked it into his armpit pouch.

“It’s the best rock I have ever seen!” he said.

What Otter found

Review: After reading

Use your assessment from hearing the children read to choose any GPCs, words or tricky words that need additional practice.

Read 1: Decoding

- Look together at page 15. Ask the children to find the two words that contain the /ow/ sound (*found*, *brown*). Point out that the spellings are different. (*ou*, *ow*)
- Challenge the children to find some other words with the /ow/ sound spelled "ou" in the story. (e.g. *around*, page 10; *pouch*, page 21)

Read 2: Prosody

- Model reading each page with expression to the children. After you have read each page, ask the children to have a go at reading with expression.
- Show the children how you take the part of narrator or Otter and demonstrate how you give life to the characters.

Read 3: Comprehension

- Look together at pages 22 and 23. For every question ask the children how they know the answer. Ask:
  - What are these things?
  - What did Otter think they were?
- What problem does Otter have in this story? (*he loses his rock*)
- Which two creatures would hurt Otter if he put them in his pocket and why? (*the crab and the urchin, because they were sharp*)
- Which part of the story do you like best, and why?